Even the Dead

POEMS, PARABLES AND A JEREMIAD

JEREMY CRONIN

MAYIBUYE BOOKS
University of the Western Cape

DAVID PHILIP PUBLISHERS
Cape Town Johannesburg

First published 1997 in Southern Africa by David Philip Publishers
(Pty) Ltd, 208 Werdmuller Centre, Newry Street, Claremont, 7700,
and Mayibuye Books, University of the Western Cape, Private Bag
X17, Bellville, 7535, South Africa

© Jeremy Cronin 1997

ISBN 0 86486 336 5

Mayibuye History and Literature Series No. 77

Typeset by User Friendly
Printed and bound by Clyson Printers, 11th Avenue, Maitland, Cape
Town, South Africa

Contents

Explaining Some Things

THREE REASONS FOR A MIXED, UMRABULO, ROUND-THE-CORNER POETRY

i.
A poem is meant to stand upon its own
Like a Grecian urn in some colonial museum,
The object of a contemplation
(Thou still unravish'd bride ...) that obscures:

     The mud of its production;

     The complicity in our gaze.

ii.
Between, let's say, May 1984 and May 1986
(Speaking from my own limited, personal experience,
  of course)
There was a shift out there
From lyric to epic.

iii.
Our contemporary, the great northern Ireland poet,
Writes from within and for
A culture that assumes Homer, Spenser, Yeats.

I live in a country with eleven official languages,
Mass illiteracy, and a shaky memory.

Here it is safe to assume
Nothing at all. **Niks.**

RUNNING TOWARDS US

It's two days after the worst. We've just returned from Johannesburg. We drop comrades in the vicinity, and decide, as Trevor puts it, to have a look.

Along roads pitted with the remains of barricades, swerving and bumping we go, eyes unpeeled.

Mahobe Drive has become a patrol strip. Armoured personnel carriers move up and down its half kilometre. They ignore us. Or, perhaps, they are watching closely. The hooded, slit-windowed faces of the vehicles make us uncertain. We don't linger.

Mahobe Drive is the cut-line, beyond it: ash and buckled zinc as far as the eye sees. 80 dead, I have read. 2 000 shacks destroyed. 20 000 homeless. Dull numbers to guess three days of devastation that have just happened here.

In those three days the apartheid police and army have destroyed an entire shanty-town, unleashing black vigilantes (witdoeke), victims themselves turned perpetrators, to perform much of the dirty work.

After-shocks, neuralgic points, are all around us now. An old man stumbles along with a corrugated sheet of zinc on his back. His eyes are blank with terror. He is half running, but from whom, and to where?

Over by the church, which will itself be burnt down in the coming days, there is a milling of refugees. People are jumpy. Suddenly from their skittish midst a sprinting of three, twenty, some sixty youth hurl themselves off in a wheeling pursuit. Or are they fleeing?

We shouldn't, shouldn't be here.

Around the corner are the New Crossroads homes, formal structures, the last line of sanctioned black poverty before ground zero, the burnt-out acres of the shanty-town.

As we turn the corner, we see people in their front yards
watching a strip of empty veld. There is a corpse lying there.

It moves. One knee bends and keels over.

Across the field, a young man draped in a blanket approaches
the body. Casually he places sticks on its chest. Another figure
strolls up to dowse the body with petrol.

All of this is done unhurriedly. In broad daylight. In the middle
of an open field, before some hundred people, and around the
corner from the police and army.

The lackadaisical visibility of this execution is, must be, the
main point.

The executioners preparing the victim move back and forth,
leaving him untended for many minutes at a time. This is ritual.
A macabre human sacrifice on the lip of a still smouldering
volcano, as if to stake challenge to its monopoly on death.

The car tyre, that will burn and burn, immolating the victim in
its rubbery inferno, is now being rolled out and placed on his
chest.

Let's go! Please! I am pleading with Trevor. The words I have
been reciting finally spilling out.

But is it horror? Or rage at our own impotence? Or the self-
disgust of the voyeur? Or is it fear that, while we watch, we too
will be engulfed from behind, overpowered, knocked down and
carried off by the police, or the youth, or the *witdoeke*?

But now the executioners themselves are disappearing, not
running, not diminishing their authority, just melting away. The
hundred-odd observers in the front yards of their homes are
also fading off.

And just as suddenly the corpse in the middle of the field is up, and sprinting away. In our direction. A wild, hobbling dash.

The victory of life over death? Of the innocent small person caught in the middle?

But what is the middle?

Are you sure, in the thick of all this slaughter, he could be innocent?

Whom did he just betray? Whom will he still betray now as he runs away from the executioners?

Away from the spectators. Away from the police and army with fresh killings on their hands. A corpse covered in petrol, each stumbling pace one step more away from a death it has already died.

He is running towards us. Into our exile. Into the return of exiles. Running towards the negotiated settlement. Towards the democratic elections. He is running, sore, into the new South Africa. Into our rainbow nation, in desperation, one shoe on, one shoe off. Into our midst. Running.

(1986–97)

Moorage

'without tenderness, it is hell'

Adrienne Rich

MOORAGE

i.
In its own armpit, a duck drops asleep
In the wind that rootles
In thorn scrub, *duiwel se grraan*
In Jorrie Barsby's brayed words.

Seventy-year old, *visterman*,
Lifelong inhabitant of this shore.
'Were you born here?' I ask.
'No,' he replies. 'You see
That house down the road?
I was born *there*.'

Which makes distance relative,
As is time for the fish of a tree
Planted, says Barsby, as
'Shade for my old age', on this
Sparse shore where trees do not
Easily grow, and those that manage
Are soon eaten down by cows.

Which is why, years off from any shade,
Jorrie Barsby's hope
Struggles towards old age
Knee high inside of its cow proof
Fish-net cage.

ii.
To live close to every tree you had ever planted.

Our century has been the great destructor of that,
The small and continuous community, lived in solidarity
With seasons, its life eked out around
Your fore-mothers' and -fathers' burial-ground.

iii.
Where the graveyard tilts up
For the headstones to see, stone brows
Of the dead to watch
Eastward across their lagoon.

Cornelius ('Sakkie') Petersen
Is there
Inscribed among them:

> *He was a Man*
> *Who would Give*
> *His last Fish*
>   *RIP*

From beside the church with its miracle
Of one palm, above the lagoon
Engraved as Galilee on the Sunday
Mind's eye of the fisherfolk, dead and alive

Along this actual shore from where
Cornelius Petersen has long since
Landed, scaled, given the ultimate
Fish away.

iv.
We call 'nature' something,
Frail as we now know it, too, to be,
(A punctured ozone over ravished landscapes),
Something, nonetheless, more permanent,
Cyclical, more anchored, anchoring us,
The world in our minds, our minds in our bodies,
Our bodies in the world – something like this.

Nature: once touchstone of truth for the romantics.

For the modernisers: more, an untamed invitation.

For us: A weekend away in the midst of another
State of emergency.

v.
A banner? – No, you say,
It's the whole lagoon
That flaps out sunset-time
From their merest ankles.
Elbows, dipped, stilt, dipped,
Knee, through the shallows
Flamingoes push their slow
Collective scaffold.

'Nature?' – we wonder,
What does that mean?
Of this place,
'It's too good to be true,' you say
As we walk the beach.

We have come to reflect
On struggles in places
We have left behind
And end up speaking
Mostly of here and things

Where, listen, below
The fiscal shrike's
Squelchy-boot call it's
So quiet you can hear
The small craft
Puppy-keen, straining at moorage
Each with its own wet
Chop-licking side slaps.

When, along the beach, a dark

Woman, like an apparition, it's true,

Emerges, she asks, earnestly,

Hoping, I guess, against hope

Two older companions, women, laughing behind her,

She asks: Excuse me, we were arguing,

It's too good to be true, they say.

So are you:

Illicit lovers, newlyweds, or on a weekend fling?

vi.
Ask the stream of conscience
That feeds the lagoon.
For conscience is no puritan,
It is hope, sweet water

Rinsed, wrung, spilling,
Water gargled through rock,
Than a frog puddle growing
Both more now, and
        Quieter.

Clear-eyed enough for the sky
To swallow this stolen
Glimpse of itself,
Ringed with palmiet,
Hidden in a tumble of rocks

Stay true, true, being
The hardest of struggles, stay true to your hopes,
Where the pool drops asleep
On a blink.

vii.
Or perhaps answers lie, blazon-wise,
In the item by item celebration of desire?
But not with the poet's gaze travelling over
A Grecian urn displayed in an imperial museum,
A plundered object for contemplation, nostalgia, or regret.
Not the female form alone, but
Our bodies, equal, vulnerable, conjugal, as in:

9

Entwined, nudged from under the tent's flap,
Our toes, before which, into air, clicking with static,
Tiny grasshoppers spring
Nitpicking, fine combsteeth.

As in: your eyes, stone green, going
Squigged up
When you laugh.

As in, ribbed
Are a sand-dune untouched;
A slip-way; to your tongue
The roof of my mouth.

As for the two round
Apples of your bum –
I think of the words of Oscar Mpetha
Spoken of other matters, and for another occasion,
– Comrades, he said, things start at the front, but
Everything must come from behind.

viii.
Fact: native North Americans fashion small nets
With feathers and shells
Which they suspend to trawl over sleepers:
To restrain nightmares and to glean,
From physical space, symbolic meanings.

ix.
Facing aft, then,
Back to deep waters,
Rowing like hell to get
The trek-net in place,
The spotter high on hill
Flag and whistle
Sends me out,
Pursuing an elusive
Darting of a shoal desired
That only I can catch

10

But only he can see.
And you are the one
Ankle deep in sand
Who holds to basic truths
Like the rope
Of the net's beginning.

Between the spotter
And yourself
Oarwood chafed in rowlocks
Here I am.
You insist on back.
The spotter waves me on.

x.
Gulled to disputation
Into every footprint we press
Some anger,
Into the headwind,
As we track in confusion, along the beach
Our separate, together, unreconciled ways,
Embroiled in our wrangles,
Our ravelling unpeelings,
Over the bones of us,
Over the pickings.
– God let us hold
Some certainty, our gull's hearts
Cry out – Enough.
Enough – raucously. Swivel-bodied, scavenger,
Skew on into the wind,
Or let us fall
Falling away
As suddenly, wind with the wind to within
One swoop of a
Centimetre
Over the hummocky sand.

xi.
Chock full,
With hidden motive
Is the rock pool.

Where under the lash of wave, overspilling,
Hard-case, recidivists, the barnacles
Knuckle down.

But closing, oh, its eyes with each,
To make a clean breast of it, with each
Wave the beach sighs: Kiss my belly, kiss ...

And everything about the way the whelk walks proclaims
Though the shell be firm
The flesh is willing.

xii.
So what are we attempting in this inter-tidal place
Of infatuation, erotic love, comradeship, quarrelling,
    companionship, back to infatuation again, or
All the way down to some future low water mark of
For the sake of the kids?

Is it the improbable notion to anchor
At the anchorage of carnal love,
Between two consenting adults,
A social scaffold called: family?
This entity of cooking, shopping, paying of bills,
Reproduction, the joint dodging of security police, and the
    rearing of kids?

For the record,
Without irony nor sense of moralising,
This IS the notion
We are attempting to live.
A small community at a biological moorage,
Or, I suspect you'd insist, the other way around.
Either way. Either way it is tenuous
Till death, and perhaps even beyond it,
Do us part.

xiii.
Because the struggle we haven't, in fact,
Left behind, as it flaps out
As this banner
Is also a struggle to make
The too good to be true be true.

Isn't it? Hmmm? We ask
In our hearts, thumping
Like small craft, puppy-keen
As we walk in our bodies.

Our biological moorage
To birth, love, death, that we push
In time always, and yet
Through all human times, stretched out
From toe to lip,
Like conjugal bodies
Affirming, something, moving now towards
Unabashed romantic closure,
Lagoon and land lie alive to and
Touching each other every
Inch of the way.

MAY DAY 1984

Epping Industrial, in your empty field by Langa station,

In your Cape Flats sands, by those four well-trod paths that move towards work

Security arc-lights dim down now in the ground-hugging mist

At 6.30, on this, rainy autumn morning, it is, and still dark.

Along the paths, for those in whose tread and march, my theory says, the future lies,

Moving in huddles which become 2, 3, 5 separate individuals only when less than ten feet off, as they pass,

Grabbing indifferent, or friendly, with a nod of recognition or a silent get stuffed.

I'm handing out a pamphlet, unbelongingly, longingly, 'Let us win May Day as a public holiday!' it says,

As an old man comes by, with a limp and a slouch.

Another, head recessed into coat collar, has, down his pipe-bowl, this thumb, tucked in fast.

Three women walk quickly, making sleepy laughter from inside of there, I mean, beneath their collective hood.

A youngster, dreadlocks a-bob, runs to beat the clock.

Whoaa, hokaai! I want to say. No,

Run on, wheel in the day, make laughter, limp, limp, limp on, tata,

May your thumb

Hold the warmth.

There was a new English in the air
As mass-based organisations sprang up
And nouns turned into verbs.
'We haven't **caucused** it yet', 'Who's **chairing**?',
'We must **workshop** this thing.'
There was a rush of acronyms:
AZASO, COSAS, GWU, CUSA, MACWUSA.
Talk of Gee-Cee's and R-Ee-Cee's,
And of Ank and Ukkas.
Syllabised words grew from initials,
Essay, the country we lived in, Sudef,
The soldiers who, one and a half years on,
Would begin to invade townships,
Door to door in pursuit
Of agitators lurking behind acronyms.
Still, Oo-Whoah remained U, double U, O:
The United Women's Organisation,
And the family circle extended, older women,
Some national figures, others grass-roots cadres,
Were known, African custom-wise, as Ma,
Or Mama (Ma Sisulu, Mama Dora),
Or Auntie (**Ooh, daai auntie kan vloek**)
When they organised on the Cape Flats.
An abbreviated **com**, for comrade, travelled
National, tongue to tongue, a small badge
Even in the most desolate, racially downtrodden
Townships of the platteland. 'Ja, com,'
People were saying, everywhere, as they shifted
The stress down to the very last syllable,
'We must orga-NISE.'

MAY DAY 1986

In the white suburbs, where I live, it is like a purloined Sunday, quiet, and with minimal traffic. But out in Bellville South, in the civic hall there is bustle. Preparations are under way for one of four trade union rallies in the Cape Town region. I'm out there with Gemma, my wife, a union full-timer. The rally is due to start in three hours.

Tchee-weep-tock-tock. The sound system is going through its testing ... One-two ... one-two ... testing. Banners are being hoisted up on walls. 'More to the right. No man, the RIGHT, ek sê!' Over there, a group of marshals is briefed. 'I want you guys to get your arses into gear. Only two accredited journalists and one photographer will be allowed in, get it?'

Now it's one hour to go. Are people coming? This is always a nervous moment for the organisers. There is news ('Man, the cops come') that the system is blocking people on their way to the meeting. 'They were driving the vans like anything. They chased us in the vans.'

At Serepta and Bellville train stations, the two nearest to the venue, workers are being forced back on to trains by the police. We also hear that workers from the Brackenfell hostels were teargassed and dispersed in the township on their way to the buses. 'The government, why she do this thing?' Two union organisers and three workers have been arrested. 'Last week it was worse. This week it will be worse, worse.'

But the hall fills up, spilling over beyond its capacity by 2.00 pm. There are songs and speeches. One group of Brackenfell workers, who have managed after all to evade the police cordon, march in, a half-hour late, singing and with banners. More speeches. More songs.

The chairperson is enthusiastic, but unaccustomed to controlling mass rallies. 'Workers and residents of Cape Town, by which I mean all of you, children of Africa ... Please, comrades, please, can I have some silence', he shouts hopelessly

16

above the singing. He clearly doesn't know the syntactic markers of a rally. Zenzo, the interpreter, moves up to assist. 'Amaaaa-ndla!', he calls, and immediately the whole hall stops short in its singing to reply: 'A-wee-thu!'.

The chairperson can proceed. 'Thank you, comrades, our next speaker is ...'

At the end, after the singing of the national anthem, and the shouting of five amandlas, five viva COSATUs, the meeting closes.

Outside the hall many of the buses for the workers from the hostels have not arrived. They've been sent back, as we later realise, by the police. On the road outside, at either end of the block, are two police Casspirs, armoured personnel carriers.

Most of the several thousand from the meeting safely leave on foot for the stations, or for the surrounding ghetto. But some hundreds of workers are stranded without buses. We mill around with them outside the hall waiting for transport. One of the police Casspirs edges forward. A metallic voice from the belly of the armoured vehicle is saying something: 'Klug – wah-wah. Klug – wah-wah.'

What?

The message is repeated, eventually becoming clearer – 'YOU HAVE THREE MINUTES TO DISPERSE!'

Suddenly there is a gun shot, **Blam!** And another, **Blam!** People edge back against the outer wall of the hall. The gun-shots turn out to be two teargas cylinders fired a little short of us, and now streaming away 40 metres off.

A delegation of three, including Gemma, moves up to the Casspir. We watch nervously. Three small figures approach the faceless, metal beast. A short exchange occurs. We can feel how their necks must be prickling now with each step, as they return, backs to an armoured vehicle laden with trigger happy police.

'The cops said they have nothing to say to us. They've ordered us back into the hall'.

People start moving back.

Suddenly – **Blam! Blam! Blam! Blam!** A volley of shots. For a paralysing moment you don't know if it is teargas, rubber bullets or hard ammunition.

It's teargas again, this time dozens of canisters right into our midst. Still more are fired, **Blam! Blam! Blam! Blam!** There is a surging, panicky push into the hall. I'm left, stuck outside. I shelter behind a side wall, out of sight from where I imagine the Casspir now finds itself. But I have badly judged where to hide. I am taking in large amounts of teargas.

Since last year they have changed its chemical composition. The people of the townships became adept at dousing themselves in water to neutralise the effects of the gas. In the big political marches and funerals last year, all along the route, township dwellers would place buckets of water, as an expression of solidarity and as a precaution. Standard gear for the young lions, the youthful activists, became a water-soaked scarf.

But this year the gas is activated by damp. It burns the moist membrane of your nostrils. It eats away at your throat. Your eyes water and that triggers more vicious stinging. You are blinded. Your nervous system short circuits, a momentary paralysis sets in. And now the stomach heaves, retching up emptiness.

Out of the mist I see a darting figure. A young kid. 'Come, com ...,' he grabs my hand, and we crouch-run for some thirty metres. 'Through here, through here,' he pushes me through a hole in the vibracrete wall around the civic hall. On the far side he asks, 'You okay, com?' I nod, feeling grateful and a little bashful at being rescued by a kid no more than ten years of age.

The run has made my stomach feel better, although my eyes are weeping, and the tears keep reactivating the gas.

I find myself in the company of four streetwise, working class kids from the neighbourhood. They take it upon themselves to escort me around. They know every wall hole and scalable fence. They know which side of a lane, being less visible, is safer. They operate like a small platoon, one scouting ahead, one watching the rear. We move across a school ground, sprinting between trees. We flatten ourselves down the side of a prefab block of class-rooms. The leader of the group squats down, getting his eyes to knee level, below the foliage-line of the surrounding scrubs.

'Daar! Daar kom hulle. Don't run, come this way.'

This evading but staying in touch goes on for some 40 minutes.

I'm anxious that the comrades in the hall might be concerned about me.

It turns out that I am one of the lucky ones. The few hundreds who got back into the hall, were then shut in. Volleys of teargas were fired into the hall, and then gas-masked police charged in with quirts, viciously whipping choking people, young and old, men and women. Gemma has three large, bleeding weals across her thighs.

******

That was our May Day 1986. A small episode in a countrywide action that turned out to be the biggest, to that date, political strike in our country's history. The people had proclaimed their own pubic holiday. Some two and a half million workers and students were involved.

The next day in their editorials, the newspapers congratulate the authorities for showing a more than customary restraint.

THE MIRACLE OF FISHES

You said:
It's the fault of a handful of agitators.

The agitators said (they liked to quote Mao):
We are fishes.

Meaning, in a sea that was us,
The great majority, the excluded-included.

Settled, unsettled, resettled beyond your horizons,
Beyond the rail-tracks and the ring of free-ways.

Far enough, but close enough,
To be labourers, domestic workers, Pep Store consumers.

Scattered, but crammed together,
Dispersed from your power centres,
We were regimented and encircled.

So we turned these exclusions
Into places of empowerment.
The township, the bush college, even the prison yard
Became
School for cadres.

Of us, you said: They are foreigners.

But still you solicited our custom.
Daily you wheeled us
Through the portals of the city.
We were Greeks,
You supplied the wooden horses.

For a day, or days, or weeks
We rejected these third class inclusions.
We declared stayaway.
We boycotted buses, shops, dummy elections.

We demanded a real say, but always you declined.
So we turned micro-space into parliament.

Umrabulo ruled in the street committee,
Debate raged through SRCs, and church halls,
Even the burial ground became
Lekgotla.

You called this communism
(You were more profound than any of us realised).

You called it:
        Total Onslaught.
You unleashed:
        Total Strategy.

The violence which had always
Pressed down upon us
Now came in through the windows
        Of our township trains,
        Of the very rooms where we slept and held vigil.

You recruited pseudo Greeks,
Green Beans, Black Cats, Witdoeke, Askaris.
These were infiltrated into the bellies
Of the wooden horses.
Cynically you called the result
Black on black violence.

In this way you applied
The Pentagon maxim:
If you can't catch the fish, poison the waters.

But still, still we resisted.

What began when you said
It's just a handful of agitators,

Ended in this:
We, the great majority, the excluded-included became
30 million local councillors,
30 million parliamentarians,
30 million agitators.

        The miracle of the multiplication of fishes.

POEM IN A SMALL FIST
(for G and B)

Erasing distance
Between the pleasure and its sign
At the breast our newborn enacts
The utmost beginning of every
Lyrical poem in his fist

That clasps and unclasps
As it floats along
With its cattail's wisp
And his whole snuffling soul weighs down
Into his lipples

But above
Is his fist
As closest to not being after as could be as any
Rippling
After-trace on pleasure.

　　　　　　* * * * * *

Tracked and wanted
On the run for two years
My mug shot
On their charge-office walls

In the depths of their emergency
Benjy's fist
Is this flag

Our own in its way
Raised up to say
This is a people's war.

We shall wage it
As people.

(Cape Town, mid-1987)

22

ON WATCH

i.
Home, almost it could be, home,
As the frog's call runs a small finger
Up and down, grook-grick-grook,
Tonight's gap-toothed comb.

The dirty war has receded, for the moment,
Unlikely, so I reckon, they will come
As a raiding party, gung-ho, this night,
Faces blackened and dark bandanas,
Dead of night, or later, if airborne,
Chopper blades churning first light.

All of this, which has happened
Here and hereabouts before,
Is unlikely tonight. Nonetheless,
Pen in hand, poem on page,
At my feet a Kalashnikov – broad
Strategic calculations notwithstanding.

Grook-grick-grook, and then
Dawn. And zick. The lights go down,
Stars slink off, same with the moon
Leaving behind its one pale, bloep,
Thumbprint, stuck to the sky.

ii.
Christ is the Answer is the banner
Corner Kwacha Road. The question
Is less obvious. Unless it be the 'Rock of Ages'
Minibus that teeters round
The self-same corner with its too many,
My own uncertainties, hanging on,
Like an abnormal load.

Exile means this. Not knowing
The question, nor getting beyond
The surface of Lusaka's dusty signs, this one
Proclaims: **Ministry of Decentralisation. HEADQUARTERS.**

Or the child's kite above the squatter camp.
Patched from a thrown-away plastic bag,
Yearning at a string, between
This sky and this Fourth World.

I'm sick of exile, says Themba Miya.
I want to be home, where I can
Catch hell (and throw some).

(ANC IPC House, Lusaka – mid-January 1990)

AND WHAT'S BECOME OF?
(for K and F)

... And so and so?
It's the last night of her stay,
So we reach into our lives,
Our way of affirming
Faith to each other,
Touching the discontinuous
That only we now seem
To hold together
In this what's become of?
Those we knew together,
Who have gone off
Into other lives.
Or who've simply
Gone. Like her husband, who I hear
For the first time now
Was dying for two years, and he knew it,
And she knew it, and I didn't, which casts
A whole different light
Upon my sunny eighth and ninth
Years upon this earth
Just as my five-day's old daughter's birth
The reason for my mother's flying visit
(Which is coming to an end this night)
Casts, upon all those that only we now
Hold together in this last night's recollecting,
Casts her only-just, her flickering,
Five-day's old life's sacred light.

(Johannesburg, July 1991)

25

THIS CITY

Joburg's high summer packs tall clouds aloft
As we drift into never-never,
Windows uptight, door-knobs down.

It's Mozart, commuting through the littered streets,
On my car stereo, through this unlovely town.
The heart torn out, suburbed, scattered, shopping-malled,
And beyond are the dark moons:
Alexandra, Thembisa, Vosloo, Soweto.

I live in the inner suburbs where
Endangered, the panting lupus, *pasop vir,*
Has long since staged a domestic return,

And our own privatised armed responders,
The very ones, perhaps, whose coming
In Lusaka once I feared, are now
A mere touch-pad in our night away.

This is a screwed-up, wounded city, bruised
By the abusings of its past,
Stoop-shouldered, hard-talking, vulgar,
Gauteng's (you have to hawk to say that) epicentre,
One of the one hundred big cities of the globe.

To live in this unchosen place is to choose
A city among cities, like a Seoul or Sao Paulo,
Where, despite it all, the working people
Still possess capacity and motivation
To shake and shake and shake the coming age.

Here we live. Here, where without
Compassion, comradeship, tenderness
        It is hell.

(Johannesburg 1997)

Even the Dead

JOE SLOVO'S FAVOURITE JOKE

It's Cuba, you know, 1959. The guerrilla forces have just taken power, and there is a hurried meeting of the leadership in the newly liberated Havana. Afterwards, shaking his head, a bewildered Che Guevara takes his friend aside: 'Comrade Fidel, why on earth have you made me Minister of Banking?'

'Well, you put up your hand when I asked: Who here is an economist?'

'Oh my no-o-o,' groans Che. 'I thought you asked: Who here's a COMMUNIST?'

******

The struggle calls for more than laughter.
But also laughter. History can advance on its funny side
By freak, frailty and unplanned – Joe understood that.

As he understood the imperative of the plan,
Decisive action, the general line, which is why

In the last years of his life, it wasn't the collapse
Of the wall of stone certainty alone,
But something deep in his personality

That led him to recommend both
Socialism and the market.

I imagine now him saying: The plan
Is the plan, and the market
          Is a joke.

Under capitalism – a bad joke.
          Under socialism ...
                    who knows?

28

FIVE THOUGHTS CONCERNING THE QUESTION: 'WHAT HAPPENS AFTER MANDELA GOES?'

1   With the words 'after' and 'goes'
The question at least proves
We are not living in a theocratic dynasty like, say,
North Korea's.

2   He stands on an ancient threshold.
One foot in the commune, one foot
In a once barely emergent aristocracy.
No easy walk.
And so he walks, stolid, uneasily-easily,
Through this cynical end of the 20th century,

Ranging the globe with arcane values:
Of honour, pride, stubbornness, dignity
And a tradition of leadership to be earned
Only in daily communion with a people.

3   Something like all of this could get lost
After Mandela goes.

4   From an organisational viewpoint,
'What after?' betrays another anxiety.

'There is only one-one-ONE ANC,' I've been told.
I agree, provided
The next question isn't:

Whose?

5   For the sake of democracy
These words should be thoroughly mistrusted:
'Identity'; 'we have always', and 'in the image of'.

Not to mention:
'Crown prince'.

POEM FOR MANDELA

It's impossible to make small-talk with an icon
Which is why, to find my tongue,
I stare down at those crunched-up,
One-time boxer's knuckles.

In their flattened pudginess I find
Something partly reassuring,
Something slightly troubling,
Something, at least, not transcendent.

A REPLY TO PABLO NERUDA

It is true, Lautaro
Survived cascades, thorns, crags,
Slept under the sheets of snowdrifts, and
Emerged from his trials a formidable hero.

But it was only then
The Araucanian chieftain's
Fuller education began.

He had to compel himself now

To train his ear in the tree of sympathy,
To draw knowledge from small pots,
To acknowledge his debt to those many years younger.

A fearless campaigner,
A sjambok's blow in the face of injustice,
He had to learn now
The harder things

To respect the majority,
To habituate his feet to the ways of the people,
To acquire the humility in the hop of a sparrow.

He bathed himself, reluctant at first, in the waters of
    consultation,
He learned nothing can be won except by the masses.

He taught his heart to despise self-serving servitude to the
    people,
He instructed his tongue in the difference between we-simple
    (meaning us), and we-royal (meaning I).

He came to accept that this was more than a question of
    grammar.

He quarried in the mud pit of history,
He acknowledged that those hardened in struggle can end up
    with stone hearts.

He pitied the baobab.

He discovered a mandate is a weapon, not a limitation.
He sharpened his critical eye first in his own mirror.
He counselled others to mistrust claims, especially his own, to
being infallible.

He grasped the dangers of speaking alone to the python.
He noted the guile of the enemy.
He stopped underestimating the alligator's intention.

Slowly, he accepted noble suffering was not enough.

He learnt everything remains impermanent.

He realised leadership is not enlightened patronage, nor the
balancing of factions.

He took time to grasp that those most flattering to his own
vanity, were those most unreliable.

In short,

Lautaro came to understand

Surviving trial by fire, exile, stone, limitless time, or steel bars is
only the beginning of being

Worthy of the people.

THE TROUBLE WITH REVOLUTIONISM

We were so seized with revolution
We entirely forgot reform ...

Of family, work-place, bureaucracy, police force ...

Having abolished the bosses,
We became the bosses.

(In the name of the workers, of course.)

THE TROUBLE WITH REFORMISM

Politics is
Not the science of the probable,
Not the struggle for the desirable.

We scoffed at anything out of ordinary.

Politics, we said, is the art of the possible.
We are artists, and our craft:
      Embroidery.

THE TROUBLE WITH CERTAIN MARXISTS

Time passed on this earth as we debated
The ultimate step into socialism.
A generalised crisis? Elections? Insurrection?

We were experts on the final moment.
And time passed. And we debated.

EPITAPHS

For a Stalinist
Here lies an immortal brain
. Long before death
It was a mausoleum

For a Finance Minister
Grounded, here lies our beloved minister
Propagator of the Passenger
Theory of Propulsion

He asked us to tighten belts
Not because of, but in order to

Take off

For an ultra-leftist
She lived each passing Year
In the Duty-Free Zone
Though
Always with Much to Declare

For the True Source
Of the Unnamed Source
Deeply Missed
Here
In Death as in Life
Lies
BRAZENLY

A Journalist

For a recently Departed
Soul from the new Patriotic Bourgeoisie
Hey, man, don't weep
I can't take your call presently
As I'm upwardly mobile

Please leave your prayer
After the beep

For the writer of Epitaphs
You who pass by now pause and ponder

Here lies
Jeremy Cronin

Who could possibly have wished this untimely death?
I wonder

THE TIME OF PROPHETS

Through the first half of the 19th century, the Xhosa peoples bore the brunt of a British colonial army of occupation. For a people for whom war was, at most, cattle raiding, in which the defeated were readily absorbed into one's own tribal structure, the experience of total war was new, incomprehensible and terrifying. Crops were laid waste; hundreds of square miles of land seized; men, women and children annihilated. There was nothing in the old beliefs to explain, let alone ward off this catastrophe.

In May 1856, a young woman, Nongqawuse, went to draw water at the Gxara stream. She met four young men. They were the spirits of the dead, eternal enemies of the colonial settlers. They had come from battle-fields beyond the seas to aid the Xhosa people.

Nongqawuse's uncle, Mhlakaza carried the message to the paramount chief, Kreli. The spirits had given orders that all cattle, the great wealth of the Xhosa people, were to be killed and that no-one was to cultivate the land. Then, on a certain day, millions of fat cattle would spring out of the earth and great fields of corn, ready for eating, would appear. At the same time the sky would fall and crush the whites and with them all those blacks who had not obeyed.

With the full support of Kreli, the cattle-killing began almost immediately. There were believers and doubters, but the ranks of the believers steadily swelled. According to a contemporary European observer, writing a few months after the start of the cattle-killing: 'I think not less than three or four hundred thousand cattle have been killed or wasted.'

On the day designated for the miracle the sun rose in the east. It reached high noon. In the evening, as Ifubesi the owl stirred in his bush, the sun set behind a veil of mist in the west. Nothing, nothing untoward had happened. Famine deepened in the land.

However, not everyone was a loser. The labour shortage in the white settler farms and towns of the Cape Colony was alleviated. There would be other armed struggles, but the early tribal resistance of the Xhosa peoples had now been irreparably shattered.

******

These things had been heard in this land before

Midwives remembered the name Nongqawuse

Elders in the villages whispered of the cattle-killing

But our virtual-reality, modern-day soothsayers, living in global time, were oblivious

As they scanned the banking journals and followed the futures markets.

They sniffed out statistics and tut-tutted over our latest world-competitiveness ratings.

Each one had his or her own diagnostic

Yet everyone simply confirmed a consensus.

We had to send the right signals,

We had to appease the markets, a great sacrifice was required.

Every failure was attributed, in a frenzy of reproach, to conflicting signals, insufficient resoluteness, to the breaking of ranks.

Anthropologists objected.

This hysteria, they said, was the symptom of cultural stress.

This was a moment in which, old models having failed, one could fear a switch from secular to sacred.

37

The historians said this was a period of transition, a time in which there was danger leadership would pass to prophets, the Nxeles, firebrands, eclectics who talked in formulaic tongues, who brooked no contradiction, who opined with the arrogance of neophytes.

But these observations were brushed aside.

The diviners presented themselves not as high-priests, but as economists in communication with the mysteries of stock market sentiment.

The shade of Nongqawuse tried to speak out, a second time, now in warning, this time more soberly,

But neither she nor the midwives were consulted, the elders were ignored, the plight of the unemployed young bypassed, historians and anthropologists were scoffed at.

Despite moral intuition, commonsense and ancient wisdom, despite concrete evidence,

Despite great tragedies across our borders, the cosmology of the World Bank prevailed.

It was called belt-tightening, deregulation, shock therapy, wage restraint, privatisation, it was called becoming competitive, it was called a winning-nation formula.

The time of a new cattle-killing was at hand.

EVEN THE DEAD

Walter Benjamin:
'There is a secret agreement between past generations and the present one. Our coming was expected on earth. Like every generation that preceded us, we have been endowed with a form of Messianic power, a power to which the past has a claim. That claim cannot be settled cheaply.'

******

Every week I read the back page of *Martin Creamer's Engineering News*, profiles of business leaders. Last week it was the turn of:

Full name: Joggie Heuser
Position: Chief Executive of Soekor
Date and place of birth: May 1938, Bloemfontein
Education: Kroonstad High, 1955; B Comm, Pretoria 1960
Value of assets under your control: More than R1-billion
Hope for the future: For all South Africans to bury the past unconditionally ...

******

It's Johannesburg 1996. It's FW De Klerk. He's addressing a breakfast meeting of the American Chamber of Commerce.

It's in the same week of another week of the Eugene De Kock trial. Tortures, Third Force hit squads, mutilated bodies.

And it's the same story in the same week of another week of the Truth and Reconciliation Commission.

In this same week, then, De Klerk is telling the American Chamber of Commerce: 'Nowhere else in Africa will you find a country in which five large domestic banking conglomerates hold the savings of the population. In no other African country will you find such a developed insurance industry.'

And De Klerk smiles, the practised smile of the practised speaker, to signal joke coming up.

'People talk a lot about a Third Force,' De Klerk says with a twinkle in his eye. 'But in South Africa, the real Third Force is the private sector.' Unquote.

******

That was in May.

In June, the *Financial Mail*, in its *Did You Hear* column, has another little joke – and I quote: 'Scheduled SABC2 coverage of the Truth Commission was dropped on Sunday and replaced with a programme called *Circus on TV*. Did anyone notice the difference?' (Snigger) Unquote.

These civilised sneers that allow themselves to slip out on the fun pages of the financial press, or at breakfast meetings, or up there on the 20th storey, in the corridors, where they feel safe and among themselves.

******

I am not sure what poetry is. I am not sure what the aesthetic is. Perhaps the aesthetic should be defined in opposition to anaesthetic.

Art is the struggle to stay awake.

Which makes amnesia the true target and proper subject of poetry.

Amnesia, we are told, exists across two axes – the paradigmatic and the syntagmatic – as a similarity disorder, or as a contiguity disorder.

******

Amnesia is when General Geldenhuys tells us the apartheid armies were never defeated at Cuito Cuanavale.

To prove his point, the general in his memoirs superimposes a diagram of a rugby field on to a map of southern Angola. Here is one set of poles, up here at Cuito. And here are the other poles, down here on a line that runs through Jamba, Sloma, all the way into Zambia.

40

With a rugby field tilted south-east like this it's clear, when
General Geldenhuys was pushed due south all the way down to
and over the Namibian border – that wasn't part of the game, it
was off the field.

The variant of amnesia is easily diagnosed in this case.

Severe paradigmatic amnesia.

The general believes it was rugby he was playing.
       ******

But it was golf, and it was amnesia,

When the Little Maestro, Gary Player, acknowledged his British
Open victory, saying South Africa's sporting achievements are
impressive indeed considering 'we only have three million
people'.
       ******

It wasn't rugby.
       It was golf.
              And it isn't, above all,
       A whole new ball-game now

Because past dispossession still pays the dispossessor
       In compound interest

Apartheid still declares
       An annual dividend

Soekor retains R1-billion assets
       Whose origins have been buried
       Unconditionally
       ******

It's syntagmatic amnesia (container for contained) when the
official journal of my organisation, the African National
Congress, salutes the inauguration of President Mandela with a
cover, 'Free At Last!', and whoossssh, 6 Impala jets flying over
the Union Buildings. 'Free At Last!', it proclaims, forgetting to

ask – who pilots the planes?

It's amnesia when the SATV launches itself into the new South Africa and lands
    In Las Vegas
        (Ongoing, chronic, paradigmatic amnesia)

Amnesia is the fate of the 46 who were killed in Johannesburg
    But not
        Outside of Shell House
    On the day of the so-called Shell House massacre

Amnesia declares a minister innocent of apartheid-era corruption because she was
    Declared innocent by an apartheid-era commission

Amnesia appoints another commission, the Lethe Commission, the Limbo Commission, Nirvana Commission, Justice van deFerred Commission

Amnesia prevails when we claim we have returned to the family of nations
    Forgetting to ask:
        Who is we?
    Forgetting to wonder:
        WHAT family?

Amnesia classifies Third World countries as 'developing'
    (structurally adjusted amnesia)

CNN is globalised amnesia

The Gulf War – lobotomised amnesia

Santa Barbara, the Bold and the Beautiful, Restless Years – the milk of amnesia

Amnesia embraces the global reality of 23 million per annum dead of hunger and hunger-related disease
That's a daily average equivalent, in fatalities, of one Hiroshima
    Buried each day

Under the cloud of amnesia

When Chris Hani was alive the newspapers described him as a
populist war-monger
When Chris Hani was assassinated the newspapers declared him
a man of peace
    (pandemic, editorial amnesia)

There is upwardly mobile amnesia
    Affirmative action amnesia
        Black economic empowerment, the world owes
me one, Dr Motlana, give me a slice of it amnesia
    (syntagmatic amnesia – an elite for the whole)

There is winning-nation amnesia
    It puts in Olympic bids

    It summits Everest and forgets to name all but one
    Of the sherpas who carried us up

Winning-nation amnesia implies
    Some win, many lose

    And where does that leave Mozambique, Zimbabwe,
    Zambia, Angola, Lesotho and Swaziland?

    And where does that leave us
        In any sustainable future?

Beware, amnesia has no cut-off date

Beware, right now amnesia is sneering at us

Up there on the 20th floor, listen, over the cocktails, the
civilised sniggers on the pages of the *Financial Mail*

After all, we're a normal society now, except, perhaps, for the
unions and the violence

Apartheid was all the fault of those bearded chaps who like to
dress up in khaki uniforms

(I mean, who else benefited?)

No need to stand before Archbishop Tutu pleading forgiveness

Heavens no

After all, who needs AMNESTY

    When there's

Blue-chip, just the ticket, deregulated, liberalised, privatised,
free market, god-given, just to please yer, property claused,
heck I worked for it all – I earned it, affirmative actioned – not
me, now in stock, just the product, your station, people of the
south, Felicia (what's my name again?), this one's for you

It's great, it's easier, I promise you, so let's hear it again from ...

Walter Benjamin:
    *'In every era the attempt must be made anew to wrest
tradition away from a conformism that is about to overwhelm it
... Only that historian will have the gift of fanning some sparks
of hope in the past who is firmly convinced that even the dead
will not be safe from the enemy if he wins. And this enemy has
not ceased to be victorious.'*